SOUND *Artistry*
INTERMEDIATE METHOD
for EUPHONIUM T.C.

PETER BOONSHAFT & CHRIS BERNOTAS

in collaboration with

DR. GAIL ROBERTSON

Thank you for making *Sound Artistry Intermediate Method for Euphonium T.C.* a part of your continued development as a musician. This book will help you progress toward becoming a more able and independent musician, focusing on both your technical and musical abilities. It offers material ranging from intermediate to advanced, making it valuable for musicians at various experience levels.

The many instrument-specific exercises in this book will help to support your personal improvement of techniques on your instrument, focusing on skills that may not always be addressed in an ensemble or in other repertoire. You will notice there are many performance and technique suggestions throughout the book. This wonderful advice has been provided by our renowned collaborative partners, as well as the many specialist teachers we worked with to create this book.

Sound Artistry Intermediate Method for Euphonium T.C. is organized into lessons that can be followed sequentially. As you progress through each lesson, it is a good idea to go back to previous lessons to reinforce concepts and skills, or just to enjoy performing the music. Exercises include Long Tones, Flexibility, Major and Minor Scales (all forms), Scale Studies, Arpeggio Studies, Chromatic Studies, Etudes, and Duets, as well as exercises that are focused on skills that are particular to your instrument. You will notice that many studies are clearly marked with dynamics, articulations, style, and tempo for you to practice those aspects of performance. Other studies are intentionally left for you to determine those aspects of your musical interpretation and performance. This book progresses through various meters and every key. Once a key has been introduced, previous keys are interspersed throughout for reinforcement and variety. In the back of this book you will also find expanded-range scale pages and a detailed fingering chart.

We wish you all the best as you continue to develop your musicianship, technique, and artistry!

~ Peter Boonshaft and Chris Bernotas

Dr. Gail Robertson has a distinguished reputation as a euphonium artist, teacher, and clinician. She has garnered worldwide attention for her leadership, work as a composer/arranger, and her musical talent. Robertson serves as Associate Professor of Tuba-Euphonium at the University of Central Arkansas. She is the Past President of the International Tuba Euphonium Association and the International Women's Brass Conference. Additionally, she is a member of the world-famous Brass Band of Battle Creek. Gail performed for ten years with the Tubafours at Walt Disney World. Robertson's euphonium of choice is a Willson 2950TA, and she plays a bronze Warburton/Robertson mouthpiece.

alfred.com

ISBN-10: 1-4706-6660-X
ISBN-13: 978-1-4706-6660-6

Instrument photos provided courtesy of Jupiter Band Instruments/KHS America

Lesson 1

DAILY ROUTINE

Start each day with a Long Tone, Flexibility, and Tonguing exercise. This routine will vary from lesson to lesson as new exercises are introduced. Always start your day by trying to achieve your best sound.

1 LONG TONES—*Use the indicated fingerings for the notes C and B♮. If your instrument has a fourth valve, it is preferred to use it for better intonation.*

2 LONG TONES: CHROMATIC

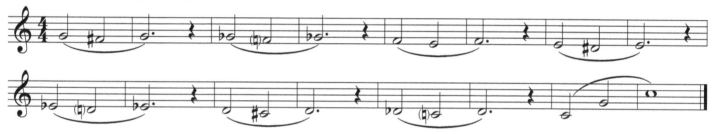

3 FLEXIBILITY

4 C MAJOR SCALE AND ARPEGGIO

5 C MAJOR SCALE STUDY

6 ARPEGGIO STUDY

7 **ETUDE**—*Play all etudes slowly with a steady tempo and good tone quality before speeding up. Always keep a good tone in mind and perform with musicality.*

Moderato ♩ = 100

8 **ETUDE**

Deliberately ♩ = 108

9 **ETUDE**—*Practice this etude with two-bar phrases and then four-bar phrases.*

Legato ♩ = 80

10 **DUET**

Majestically ♩ = 82

4

Lesson 2

11 **LONG TONES**

Play the Flexibility study from Lesson 1 before playing exercise 12.

12 **A MINOR SCALE**—*For all scale exercises that are written in octaves, practice each octave separately and then as a two-octave scale and arpeggio.*

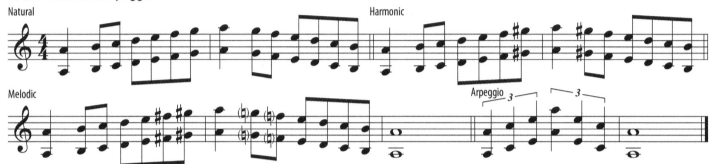

13 **A MINOR SCALE STUDY**

14 **ETUDE**

15 **ETUDE**

16 CHROMATIC SCALE

17 CHROMATIC SCALE ETUDE

Moderately ♩ = 88

18 ETUDE

Lightly ♪ = 120

19 ETUDE—*After playing this etude as written, create or improvise a new ending for the last two measures.*

Moderately ♩ = 100

Lesson 3

20 **LONG TONES**—*Remember to always have proper posture, embouchure, and hand position to promote performing with a beautiful tone.*

21 **FLEXIBILITY**

22 **G MAJOR SCALE AND ARPEGGIO**—*Sing or hum these notes before playing them. Internalizing the pitch will help develop your aural skills.*

23 **G MAJOR SCALE STUDY**

24 **ETUDE**

25 **ARPEGGIO STUDY**

26 **ETUDE**

27 **DUET**

Lesson 4

Pick a Long Tone, Flexibility, and Tonguing Study/Etude from Lessons 1–3 as your Daily Routine.

28 E MINOR SCALE

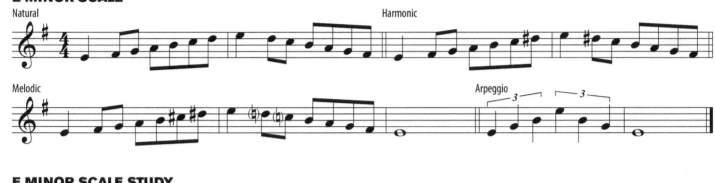

29 E MINOR SCALE STUDY

30 ETUDE

31 ETUDE

32 **DUET**—*Work towards matching each of the musical elements in this duet for a unified performance.*

33 **ETUDE**—*Play this etude with an eighth-note pulse until the rhythm is accurate. Then, transition to the dotted-quarter-note pulse.*

Lesson 5

Pick a Long Tone, Flexibility, and Tonguing Study/Etude from Lessons 1–4 as your Daily Routine.

37 **ETUDE**

Stately ♩ = 98

38 **DUET**

Maestoso ♩ = 72

39 **ETUDE**

Cantabile ♩ = 72

Lesson 6

Pick a Long Tone study from a previous lesson before playing exercise 40.

40 FLEXIBILITY

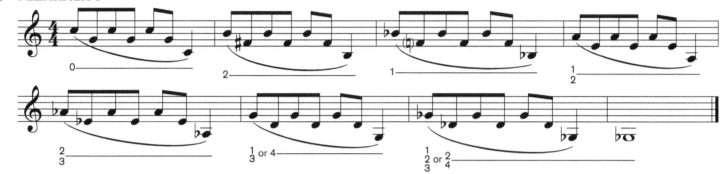

41 A MAJOR SCALE AND ARPEGGIO

42 A MAJOR SCALE STUDY—*Using manuscript paper or notation software, compose a new scale study that you think is even more challenging.*

43 RANGE EXTENSION—*Before playing this exercise, using a tuner or piano keyboard to help with finding the correct pitches, buzz this exercise on just your mouthpiece. Then play the exercise, making sure you are not rolling your bottom lip inward when playing. Keep a "poo" shape with your embouchure throughout. Once you are comfortable with this exercise, try playing it in the key of B♭ and extend the range all the way to the high B♭.*

44 RANGE EXTENSION—*When playing this exercise, make sure you keep your oral cavity (inside of your mouth) more open, as if you are saying "toe" or "tuh." If your low notes are sharp, you're likely not saying "toe." Continue to extend your lower register to pedal B♭.*

45 INTERVAL STUDY—*Once you are comfortable with this as written, practice it an octave higher. Practice this study slurred and then with legato tonguing. Always strive to play with a beautiful sound.*

46 ETUDE

47 ETUDE—*Practice this etude with two-bar phrases and then four-bar phrases.*

48 ETUDE

14

Lesson 7

Pick a Long Tone study from a previous lesson before playing exercise 49.

49 **FLEXIBILITY**

1 or 4
3

50 **F♯ MINOR SCALE**

Natural   Harmonic

Melodic   Arpeggio

51 **F♯ MINOR SCALE STUDY**

52 **ETUDE**

Majestically ♩ = 88

mf

f   *mf*

53 **COMMON FINGERS**—*Practice this exercise for third finger dexterity.*

54 **ETUDE**

55 **ETUDE**—*After successfully playing this etude, seek guidance from a teacher for ways you can refine your performance.*

56 **ETUDE**

Lesson 8

Pick a Long Tone study from a previous lesson before playing exercise 57.

57 FLEXIBILITY

58 D MAJOR SCALE AND ARPEGGIO

59 D MAJOR SCALE STUDY

Moderately ♩ = 112

60 ETUDE—*If this exercise is not rhythmically even at the dotted-quarter-note pulse, try setting your metronome to the eighth-note pulse of ♪ = 180.*

Adagio ♩. = 60

61 ETUDE—*Be creative with the musicality of this etude by altering and adding your own dynamic markings.*

Cantabile ♩ = 72

62 DUET

63 B MINOR SCALE

64 B MINOR SCALE STUDY

65 ETUDE

Lesson 9

Pick a Long Tone, Flexibility, and Tonguing Study/Etude from a previous lesson before playing this lesson.

> **GRACE NOTES** are ornaments that are performed before the beat or on the beat, depending on the musical time period, style, context, and notation. The last example below shows how unslashed grace notes would be performed in the Classical period. Listen to music from various historical periods and notice the different approaches to the performance of grace notes.
>
> Most often performed before the beat   Classical period, no slash. On the beat (in time).
>
>

66 **GRACE NOTES**—*Play these grace notes just before the main note.*

Precisely ♩ = 120

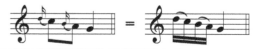

67 **ETUDE**

Moderato ♩ = 80

68 **ETUDE**—*An appoggiatura is a grace note without a slash that is played on the beat. In this exercise, measures 1 and 5, as well as measures 3 and 7, would be played the same.*

Cantabile ♩ = 72

69 **ETUDE**

Lightly ♩ = 96

70 **ETUDE**

Andante ♪ = 96

71 **ETUDE**

72 **ETUDE**—*Record your performance of this etude. Recognize the personal musical growth you have made from when you sight-read the piece. Think about the technical and musical ways your performance has improved. Do you hear a difference?*

73 **ETUDE**—*Practice this exercise with a metronome. Start slowly and gradually increase your speed. Be sure to attend to all articulations from the very first time you play the exercise! If possible, memorize the tricky passages so you are only glancing at the music as a guide.*

Lesson 10

78 **CHROMATIC SCALE**—*Practice this exercise both tongued and slurred. Exaggerate firmly pressing down the valves to keep the rhythm even.*

79 **CHROMATIC RANGE**—*Be sure to maintain good air support throughout the exercise. Practice this exercise both slurred and tongued.*

80 **MAJOR SCALE RANGE**—*Keep your body relaxed when playing in the upper register. Practice this exercise both slurred and tongued.*

81 **DUET**

Lesson 11

Pick a Long Tone study from a previous lesson before playing exercise 82.

82 **FLEXIBILITY**—*Remember that constant air support is key for exercises like this.*

83 **E MAJOR SCALE AND ARPEGGIO**

84 **E MAJOR SCALE STUDY**

Moderately ♩ = 120

85 **ETUDE**

86 **ETUDE**

Allegro ♩ = 90

mf sempre staccato

continued on
next page

87 **ETUDE**

88 **ETUDE**—*After performing this etude, discuss the various elements of the musical work with a peer or teacher.*

89 **ETUDE**

Lesson 12

Pick a Long Tone study from a previous lesson before playing exercise 90.

90 FLEXIBILITY

91 C# MINOR SCALE

92 C# MINOR SCALE STUDY—*Always use the 4th valve of your instrument, if it has one.*

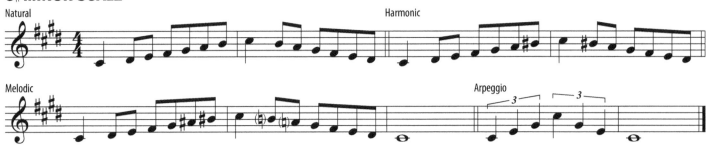

93 C# MINOR SCALE STUDY

94 DUET—*Make sure to exaggerate the dynamics in this duet.*

A **TRILL** is an ornament that is performed by alternating rapidly between the written note and the next diatonic note above. Sometimes you will see a natural, sharp, or flat sign with a trill, which means to alternate between the written note and the next altered note. Always check the key signature.

95 **TRILLS**—*Use your metronome to ensure an even and consistent rhythm.*

Evenly ♩ = 72

96 **TRILLS**—*Practice this exercise to ensure your trills are played evenly. Once you are comfortable with this exercise as written, try playing it in cut time (𝅗𝅥=160).*

Presto ♩ = 160

*Try ⅓–3

*Try ½–2

97 **TRILLS**—*Practice measures 1–5 at a slow tempo to reinforce muscle memory, gradually increasing the tempo. This exercise will help ensure that your trills are played evenly.*

Presto ♩ = 160

98 **ETUDE**—*Depending on the style or historical context, a trill may start with an upper neighbor as shown here. Practice these trills with and without the upper neighbor. Also, grace notes are often used at the end of a trill. This ornament is also known as a nachschläge. Remember to check the key signature.*

Moderately ♩ = 90

mf

Lesson 13

Pick a Long Tone study from a previous lesson before playing exercise 99.

99 **FLEXIBILITY**—*Try practicing each of these note groupings several times before moving on to the next one.*

100 **F MAJOR SCALE AND ARPEGGIO**

101 **F MAJOR SCALE STUDY**

102 **ETUDE**

103 **ETUDE**

104 DUET

Andante ♩ = 102

28

Lesson 14

105 LONG TONES

106 FLEXIBILITY

107 D MINOR SCALE

108 D MINOR SCALE STUDY

109 ETUDE

110 **DUET**

111 **ETUDE**

112 **DUET**—*While playing duets, both performers must listen critically to evaluate and adjust intonation.*

Lesson 15

Pick a Long Tone study from a previous lesson before playing exercise 113.

113 FLEXIBILITY

114 B MAJOR SCALE AND ARPEGGIO

115 B MAJOR SCALE STUDY

Moderately ♩ = 80

116 ETUDE

Moderately ♩ = 80

accel.

117 ETUDE

Cantabile ♩. = 60

Slowly

118 LONG TONES—*Add a crescendo and decrescendo as you hold each note for at least eight counts.*

Slowly ♩ = 60

119 Ab MINOR SCALE (*enharmonic spelling of G# minor*)

Natural   Harmonic

Melodic   Arpeggio

120 Ab MINOR SCALE STUDY

Andante ♩ = 88

mf

rit.

121 ETUDE

Moderato ♩ = 120

mf

p

mf

rit.

Lesson 16

Pick a Long Tone, Flexibility, and Tonguing Study/Etude from previous lessons before playing exercise 122.

122 **DUET**—*When playing ♪♪, remember to think of a sixteenth-note subdivision.*

123 **ETUDE**

124 DUET—*What musical elements in this duet make it engaging? How does the form contribute to the musical work?*

Lesson 17

Pick a Long Tone study from a previous lesson before playing exercise 126.

126 FLEXIBILITY

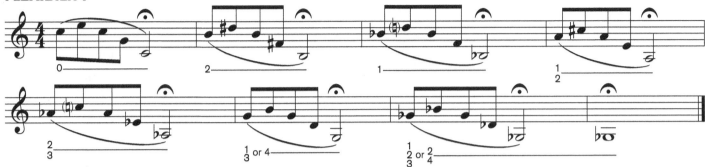

127 B♭ MAJOR SCALE AND ARPEGGIO

A **TURN** or **GRUPPETTO** is an ornament that involves playing the written note, followed by the note above it, returning to the original note, then playing the note below it, and finally ending on the original note.

128 B♭ MAJOR SCALE STUDY

Adagio ♩ = 72

129 B♭ MAJOR SCALE STUDY

Moderato ♩ = 112

130 ETUDE

Andante ♩ = 80

continued on next page

131 G MINOR SCALE

132 G MINOR SCALE STUDY

133 ETUDE

Lesson 18

134 LONG TONES

135 FLEXIBILITY

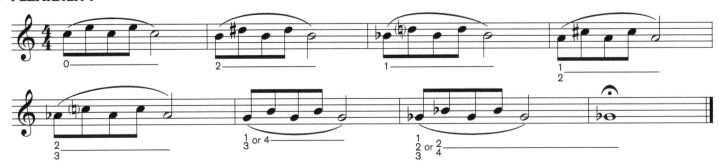

136 G♭ MAJOR SCALE AND ARPEGGIO *(enharmonic spelling of F♯ major)*

137 G♭ MAJOR SCALE STUDY

138 ETUDE

139 ETUDE

140 E♭ MINOR SCALES *(enharmonic spelling of D♯ minor)*

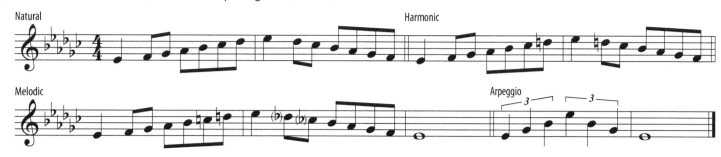

141 E♭ MINOR SCALE STUDY

142 ETUDE

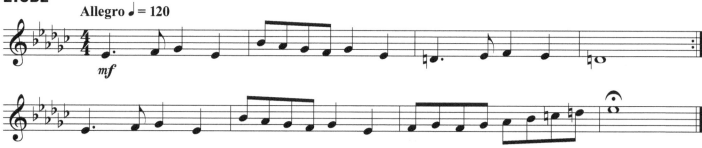

143 DUET

Lesson 19

Pick a Long Tone study from a previous lesson before playing exercise 144.

144 FLEXIBILITY

145 ETUDE

Allegro ♩ = 126

146 ETUDE

Legato ♩ = 72

147 ETUDE

Moderato ♩. = 60

148 **DUET**

149 **ETUDE**

150 **DUET**—*Use critical listening to improve the performance of all musical elements in this duet.*

Lesson 20

Fast, articulated passages often require the use of a technique called **DOUBLE TONGUING**. Double tonguing is a rapid articulation that alternates using the front/tip of the tongue and back of the tongue. Often, the syllables Tah Kah (T, K) or Dah Gah (D, G) are used to help understand the tongue placement of this technique.

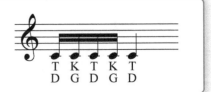

151 **DOUBLE TONGUING EXERCISE**—*For this exercise, practice four Tah articulations, then four Kah articulations, working toward making them sound the same. Then, practice double tonguing by alternating between Tah and Kah, still ensuring they sound the same. Use critical listening and experimentation to match the sound of each syllable.*

152 **DOUBLE TONGUING EXERCISE**—*As you become comfortable with this technique, increase the tempo, then perform these exercises as fast as possible. Experiment with using the syllables Dah Gah for a legato style. Apply this pattern to other scales.*

153 **DOUBLE TONGUING EXERCISE**

Fast, articulated passages in three-note groupings often require the use of a technique called **TRIPLE TONGUING**. Triple tonguing is a rapid articulation that alternates using the front/tip of the tongue and back of the tongue. Often, the syllables Tah Tah Kah (T, T, K) or Dah Dah Gah (D, D, G) are used to help understand the tongue placement of this technique. Use critical listening and experimentation to match the sound of each syllable. Triple tonguing can also be approached by using the syllables Tah Kah Tah (T, K, T) or Dah Gah Dah (D, G, D). Experiment with these various ways to see which sounds best to you.

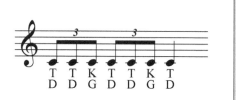

154 TRIPLE TONGUING EXERCISE—*Experiment with using the syllables Dah Gah for a legato style.*

155 TRIPLE TONGUING EXERCISE

156 TRIPLE TONGUING EXERCISE—*Apply this pattern to other comfortable keys.*

42

157 ETUDE (FANFARE)—*Practice this with both single and double tonguing.*

158 ETUDE (FANFARE)—*Practice this with both single and triple tonguing.*

159 DUET

Lesson 21

Pick a Long Tone study from a previous lesson before playing exercise 160.

160 FLEXIBILITY

161 Eb MAJOR SCALE AND ARPEGGIO

162 ETUDE

163 ETUDE

164 C MINOR SCALES

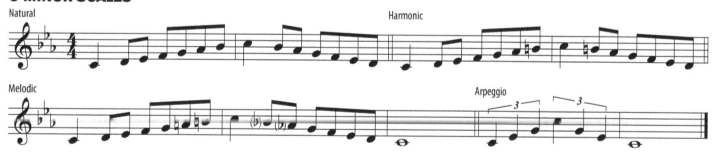

165 ETUDE

Lesson 22

166 **LONG TONES**

Pick a Flexibility study from a previous lesson before playing exercise 167.

167 **D♭ MAJOR SCALE AND ARPEGGIO** *(enharmonic spelling of C♯ minor)*

168 **ETUDE**

169 **ETUDE**

170 **B♭ MINOR SCALE**

171 **ETUDE**

Major Scales

C MAJOR

F MAJOR

B♭ MAJOR

E♭ MAJOR

A♭ MAJOR

D♭ MAJOR

G♭ MAJOR

C♭ MAJOR

G MAJOR

D MAJOR

A MAJOR

E MAJOR

B MAJOR

F♯ MAJOR

C♯ MAJOR

Minor Scales

A MINOR
Natural   Harmonic   Melodic

D MINOR
Natural   Harmonic   Melodic

G MINOR
Natural   Harmonic   Melodic

C MINOR
Natural   Harmonic   Melodic

Euphonium/Baritone T.C. Fingering Chart

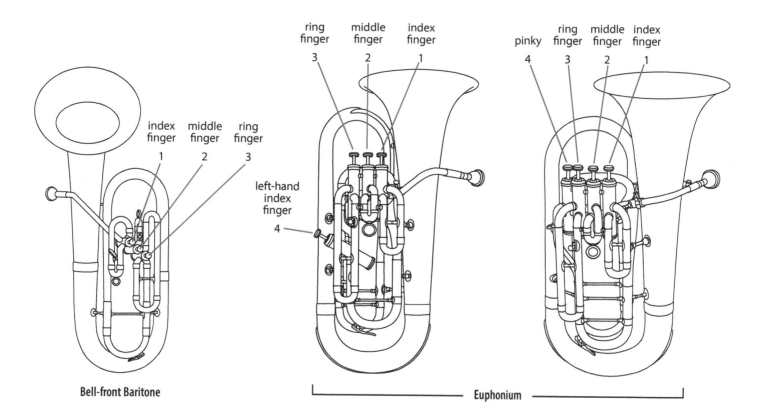

Bell-front Baritone

Euphonium

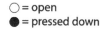 = open
● = pressed down

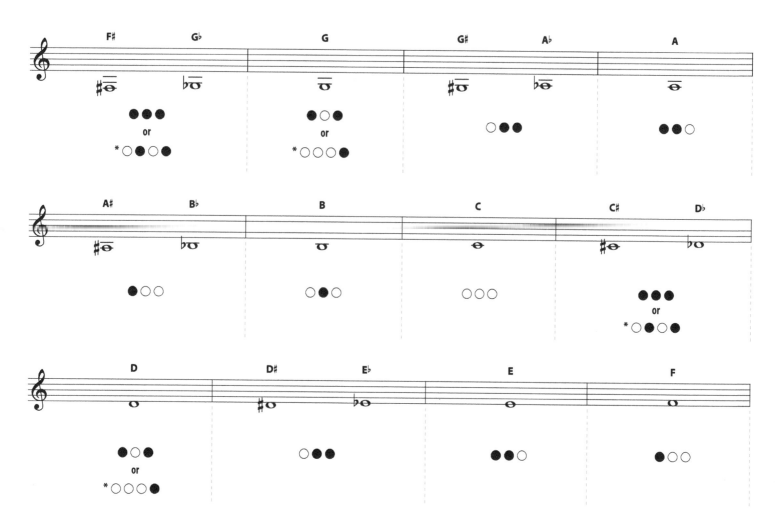

*If playing on an instrument with 4 valves, use the alternate fingering.

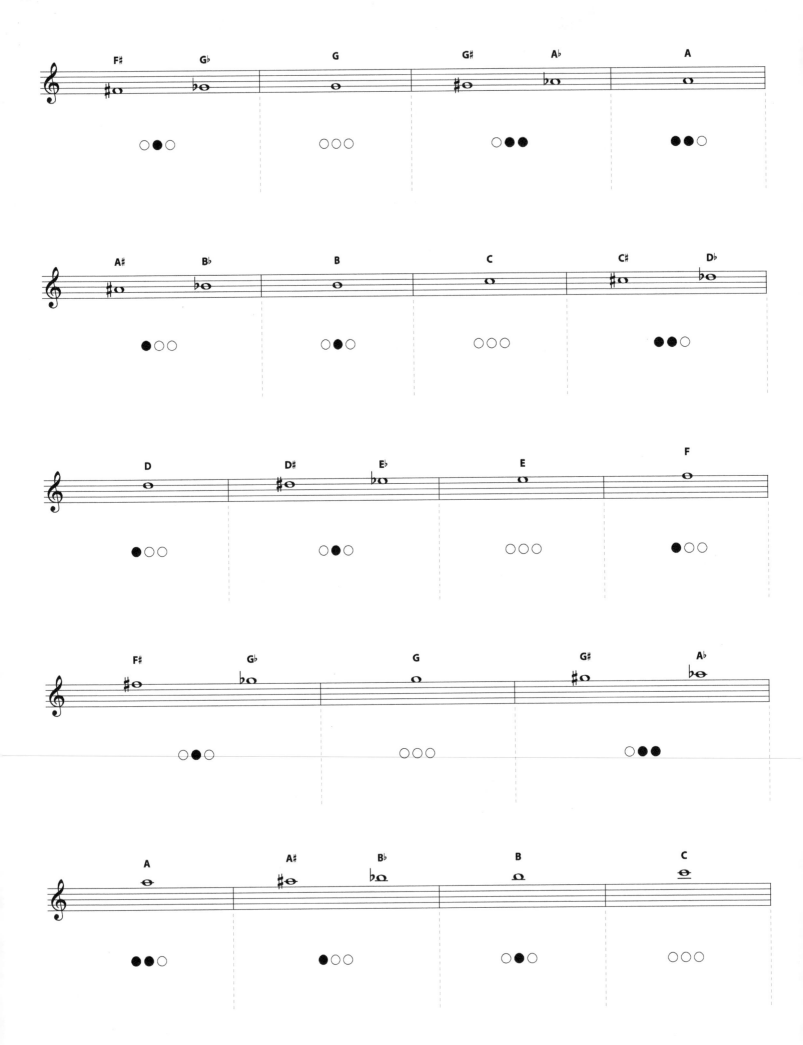